COMPANIONS OF HIS THOUGHTS MORE GREEN
Poems for Andrew Marvell

Edited by David Wheatley
With an afterword by Stewart Mottram

Anthologies from Broken Sleep Books

The Plum Review (2022)

Cornish Modern Poetries (2022)

Queer Icons: A Queer Bodies anthology (2022)

Footprints: an anthology of new ecopoetry (2022)

You have so many machines, Richard: an anthology of Aphex Twin poetry (2022)

Broken Sleep Books 2021 (2021)

Snackbox: an anthology of Legitimate Snacks (2021)

Hit Points: an anthology of video game poetry (2021)

Crossing Lines: an anthology of immigrant poetry (2021)

Broken Sleep Books 2020 (2020)

Broken Sleep Books 2019 (2019)

Broken Sleep Books 2018 (2018)

Contents

INTRODUCTION	9
IAN DUHIG	17
JASON ALLEN-PAISANT	21
TOM COOK	24
MARTIN MALONE	25
INGRID LEONARD	26
CHRISTOPHER ARKSEY	28
MARY MCCOLLUM	30
AARON KENT	31
NUZHAT BUKHARI	32
MALCOLM WATSON	34
SUNA AFSHAN	36
RORY WATERMAN	38
CAMILLE RALPHS	39
MATTHEW FRANCIS	41
CLIFF FORSHAW	43
ISHION HUTCHINSON	53
CAROL RUMENS	56
WILL HARRIS	59
EMILY BERRY	60
SEAN O'BRIEN	61
NYLA MATUK	62

ALEC FINLAY	63
ANGELA LEIGHTON	67
JUSTIN QUINN	69
JANA PRIKRYL	70
STEPHANIE BURT	72
JON THOMPSON	73
PAUL MULDOON	74
STEWART MOTTRAM	75
EILÉAN NÍ CHUILLEANÁIN	77
JOHN GREENING	79
DAVID WHEATLEY	81
AFTERWORD	83

© 2022, Broken Sleep Books. All rights reserved;
no part of this book may be reproduced by any means
without the publisher's permission.

—

ISBN: 978-1-915079-70-1

—

brokensleepbooks.com

—

The authors have asserted their right to be
identified as the authors of this Work in accordance
with the Copyright, Designs and Patents Act 1988

—

Cover designed by Aaron Kent

—

Typeset by Aaron Kent

—

Edited by David Wheatley

Broken Sleep Books
Rhydwen
Talgarreg
Ceredigion
SA44 4HB

Broken Sleep Books
Fair View
St Georges Road
Cornwall
PL26 7YH

Companions of his Thoughts More Green

Edited by David Wheatley

Introduction

— *David Wheatley*

Accounts of Hull poetry are apt to stress the end-of-the-line quality of that city – literally so in Philip Larkin's vision, in his foreword to *A Rumoured City: New Poets from Hull* (1982), of a train 'com(ing) to rest in Paragon Station against a row of docile buffers'. Yet just as there were Hull poets before Larkin and Douglas Dunn, there is more to East Yorkshire than Hull. A drive to the eerie landscapes of Spurn Point on the coast passes through a clutch of villages, among them the hamlet of Winestead, birthplace in 1621 of Andrew Marvell. Though Winestead is not on the water, the surrounding fields are sufficiently flat for passing ferries and container ships to loom up in the distance like combine harvesters, those latter-day improvements on Damon the mower. The East Yorkshire coastline is among the fastest-eroding in Europe, receding inexorably west and giving the names of its many lost villages to North Sea gas-fields. In 1641 the poet's clergyman father was drowned while attempting to cross the Humber in a barrow boat, a tragedy that ripples somewhere in the background of the lines 'I by the tide /Of Humber would complain', in Marvell's great love complaint, 'To His Coy Mistress'.

Much later, as MP for Hull, Marvell would lobby for the construction of a lighthouse at Spurn Point. Poet and politician address the vengeful tide from very different worlds, and the swallowing up of Marvell the private citizen by Marvell the public man has posed a powerful obstacle to getting this most elusive of poets into focus down the centuries. At the time of his tercentenary in 1921, he was remembered principally as a pamphleteer and defender of the parliamentarian 'good old cause'. He made himself the laureate of Cromwell's reign with his 'Horatian Ode Upon Cromwell's Return from Ireland', that most startling of political poems, pulling off the feat of marking the execution of Charles I and Cromwell's ascendancy without quite making clear which side he was on. 'The border /between the dead and us is not so hard / that you can't whisper', John Greening tells the shade of Cromwell in 'To the Lord Protector', his poem of the aftermath of civil war, and Marvell's role in imagining a new political settlement. Marvell was appointed to the Office of Latin Secretary in 1657, before his election as MP two years later. During this period he wrote much anonymous satirical verse, and found a further outlet for his love of intrigue in missions to Holland and to the Czar's court in Russia, the latter memorably described in Matthew Francis's *Muscovy* (2013). The accepted narrative of Marvell's activities in Holland was, until recently, that he had been acting as an English spy in the fevered atmosphere that surrounded the Anglo-Dutch war of 1672-4, but new research suggests he may have acted for the other side, forging an alliance with and perhaps even meeting William of Orange, later William III. He died suddenly in 1678, with an edition of his poems appearing at last in 1681, courtesy of his landlady, now styling herself the poet's widow.

Arguably, the Marvell we know today had to wait a little longer to be born – until 1921 and the publication in the *Times Literary Supplement* of a tribute by T. S. Eliot hailing Marvell as a metaphysical poet and sponsor of the modernist lyric, as practised by among others Eliot himself. Marvell was someone 'whose best verse', Eliot argued, 'is the product of European, that is to say Latin culture.' Keen to differentiate the modernist era from Victorian escapism, Eliot leaned heavily on the concept of metaphysical wit: 'more than a technical accomplishment, or the vocabulary and syntax of an epoch; it is, what we have designated tentatively as wit, a tough reasonableness beneath the slight lyric grace.' The poems that drew Marvell's new admirers were the love lyrics, the religious poems, and the garden meditations – 'To his Coy Mistress', 'The Definition of Love', 'The Coronet', 'Eyes and Tears', 'Clorinda and Damon', 'The Mower's Song' (which gives this anthology its title), 'Damon the Mower', 'The Mower Against Gardens', and 'Daphnis and Chloe', to name but some of the best-known.

Richly textured and dense with ambiguities, Marvell's poems became favourite testing grounds for New Critical close reading. The New Critical paradigm prized formal detachment over social engagement, but writing in 1978 Christopher Ricks reasserted the political uses of metaphysical wit in his study of Marvell's 'self-inwoven simile' (a drop of dew 'like its own tear'), and the copying of this technique by Northern Irish poets as a defence mechanism during a time of civil strife. Current unrest in the British body politic lends itself to Marvellian reimagining in Martin Malone's ''Tis Marvellous Strange', with glancing allusions to more pastoral spaces amid outbreaks of conflict ('We drain the fen to make our children's wars, /lack time enough and world to put it right /but cloak our woes in double-dealing cause'). Taking the measure of Marvell's influence on contemporary poetry however, as I have done in assembling these poems, I found a marked preference for the Marvell of the gardens to Marvell the political commentator. In the poems that follow there are many mowers' songs in green shades, but no 'Marvellian Ode on the Prime Minister's Return from Brussels'. Yet to frame this as a victory for private over public Marvell would be a reductive endeavour. In few poets, after all, is the public-private divide more opaque than Marvell. The celebrated lyrics, most notably 'To His Coy Mistress', are often presumed to belong to his early years, before the poet's entry into public life. (Marvell's mysteriously closed personality – described by Barbara Everett as 'self-mocking, subtle, permanently reserved' – is a complicating factor here.) If they do date from the 1640s and early 1650s, his garden landscapes are best understood as strategic retreats from war, and spaces of exotic cultivation – many Marvell poems, as Everett also notes, are collectors' cabinets, 'moments of time in which the world's "rarities" startlingly catch the light'. But that light is never without reflected glints and flashes of battles elsewhere, and so it is with modern reboots of Marvell's pastoral visions. 'To all the green, adieu', the young Marvell says in Malcolm Watson's 'The Wandering Statues of Marvell and Larkin', before announcing shortly afterwards his intention to 'Begin afresh our green conceits', the implication being they never really go away.

Gardens are not really retreats, joked Ian Hamilton Finlay, they are attacks, and Marvell's most developed poem of retreat is *Upon Appleton House*. Nun Appleton Priory was acquired by the Fairfax family on the dissolution of the monasteries, and with its tale of

Isabel Thwaites leaving the priory to marry a Fairfax, Marvell's poem seems to trace a narrative of irresistible Protestant ascent. The contemporary Fairfax, however, had refused to serve as a judge in the trial of Charles I, and resigned his commission in 1650 rather than participate in Cromwell's invasion of Scotland. Retreat is self-protection and, sometimes, political wisdom too. Battles are often fought on false premises and expectations, as in Nyla Matuk's 'An Insurrection' ('Airborne gods of an imagined purity /promised to deliver an outsized victory'), only for the conflict to end with an unexpected twist, as Marvell meets Franz Kafka. Is there a surer sanctuary than poetic form though, Stewart Mottram asks in 'In Search of Appleton' ('Yet here he found his own Eden /Among the sylvan paths untrodden'), self-consciously rebuilding Marvell's elegant stanzaic structures. In 'Rotten Appleton', Ian Duhig connects the dilapidated state of Nun Appleton Hall to its present owner's zealous interpretation of the maxim 'These Walls restrain the World without'. Without having ever lived in the property, the lord of the manor – a reclusive brewer – has prevented public access with no discernible show of care for the house itself. A very different form of retreat then: costive, enclosed, and self-serving. For Duhig, Marvell's octosyllabics are a convivial rebuke to isolationism, and his poem ends with a call for a round of drinks to release the house, if only in song, from its thralldom. Matthew Francis has also been to Nun Appleton House, where he finds 'waves cloven by the strimmer's / eardrum-rupturing jetski', and sufficient other disturbance to leave thought 'keeping its distance' in our compromised green spaces ('Appleton Revisited').

In her 'English Pastoral', Nuzhat Bukhari probes pastoral's implication in larger narratives ('The green /hallucinations /of history are still yours to reap'), too often depoliticized out of view. More comically, pastoral reinvents itself as a suburban simulacrum in Christopher Arksey's 'The Blower Against Gardens', with its fire pit and B&Q hot tub ('Weekly he vacuums the lawn till bare and clean, /scrubs the pavers so each fleck gleams'). Still on Humberside, Mary McCollum finds darker shadows along the estuary in 'blue air' ('i'm at the edge of the world//enjoying the noise from the refinery'), but unconquered spaces too in which deer still roam. By the banks of the same river, Aaron Kent's 'A Few More Years in Residence' senses environmental change and the overwhelming of the familiar ('The Humber rolls to its new owner's /rule, and he'll not know how /or why his city drowned'). Pastoral is ultimately something we experience on our pulses, as when Ingrid Leonard crosses 'generations /of grass' in a walk, absorbing the natural world into a state of deep interiority ('Do you feel water in you when the rain falls?'). In 'Emerging Moth' meanwhile, Stephanie Burt 'felt a sky /inside myself, a need /for infinite retreat', a retreat that nevertheless blossoms into a vision of secret freedoms, far from the human gaze. In 'Hibari', Suna Afshan confronts environmental precarity while managing to find resilience too ('Marvel how the mowed rail /Rose with a jaw in one clutch, / Its open heart in the other, /And still hiccuped its song'). With superficially faint praise for her trees ('They're good at being trees [...] /very slow branches saying little'), Jana Prikryl further recalibrates perspectives away from the anthropocentric in 'The Garden'. Love is one compelling reason at least for maintaining a human perspective, and it is perhaps surprising that more poets have not revisited 'To His Coy Mistress'. While that poem is most often read as a love-crossed swain's expression of impatience, it might also be interpreted as a song of resignation. Sean O'Brien's 'The Rose-Giver' inclines towards the latter mood, invoking the love lyric's conventions but wondering if we mightn't be better proceeding straight to the grave instead ('It would be foolish to suppose /That there will always be a rose /To flatter your imperious whim'). Emily Berry too is half in love with easeful death in 'Dying Leaves a Perfume' ('she loves to die /in the green grass //in transparent floods /so straight and green'). To Cliff Forshaw, in his 'In the Garden', all flesh is grass and the pleasures of embodiment close inexorably on a vision not unlike that of Larkin's 'Cut Grass' ('Your shadow boxes with you as you pass, / already long across the freshened grass).'

Marvell's living presence is not just a matter of themes or moods though, and for many poets he is above all a paragon of formal suavity, economy and grace. In 'Echo is Dumb', Eiléan Ní Chuilleanáin revisits how Marvell's voice does and does not lend itself to imitation across the centuries, in her attempts at 'miming that voice /that reasoned in the midst of noise', weighing the twin claims of reason and the noise of conflict and grief. In 'Short Song for Andrew Marvell', Justin Quinn offers a sonnet life of the poet who speaks 'in deft erasures' before settling into a face of 'broad and silent pasture, wind through flowers'. Camille Ralphs turns Marvell's dialogue poems to good metaphysical account in her 'Dialogue Between the Body and the Brain', acknowledging the snares of the flesh but declining to dematerialize it into Platonic abstraction ('Is body's suit still present, tense, /detained in nonsense by each sense?'). Paul Muldoon, long among the most Marvellian of modern poets, packs his quatrains with sly suggestiveness as Juliana and the mower pause from their labours 'atop the triangular mound /with its outcrop of hairy vetch' ('The Glow-Worm to the Mower'). Glow-worms also feature in Rory Waterman's 'Anniversary', their sudden glory not enough to dispel the inescapable sense of melancholy in the air ('You caught a shooting star, and poked /at where it was. Too late'). In her own quatrains, Angela Leighton explores not eros but thanatos in an elegy for a lost father, pushing Marvell's witty artifice to its human limits ('So I, by the waters that quarrel and kill, /stay, for contraries no war resolves' ('By the Tide of Humber')). Will Harris by contrast, in 'The Mower Redux', cuts his form to a different pattern, stating of a tree that 'Purity disturbs //it', and 'The enemy of thought //is thinking', following his abrasive line-ends to pastures new.

Marvell's poems are often imagined landscapes, notably the colonial dreamscape of 'Bermudas', and in 'Train to Cambridge' Ishion Hutchinson narrates the view from a Cambridge train window in terms of landscapes on the page ('These British fields straight out /of British poetry, bucolic green /and stunningly mediocre'), before redeeming things with a gaze of his own. In 'Triptych', Jason Allen-Paisant probes the gap between the specificity of the English pastoral tradition – its inclusions and exclusions – and its would-be universalism, keeping an ear out for frequencies that run below our human chatter, and that 'cause you to hear /the bark of the tree'. As Eliot's insistence on Marvell's Europeannness reminds us however, Marvell is more than just a bard of Albion. Perhaps the obscurest of all Marvells to a contemporary reader is the Latin poet, refreshed in translation by Tom Cook, whose 'Two Hillsides' paints a Pennine vista alive with historical memory ('Beyond the scarp, a war /Memorial'). A passing reference in the 'Horatian Ode' suggests a low opinion on Marvell's part of the Scots, but in 'The Garden' Alec Finlay channels Marvell's poem by way of a rewriting of Scots makar Gavin Douglas's 'The Palice of Honour' ('I was doing my qi- /gong in the walled garden /bathed in sun /scorchio as heaven'). Translation also features in Carol Rumens' 'A New Translation of an Epistle by Andrew Marvell', addressed to a Hull physician. A plague epidemic swept England in the 1630s, and may have killed Marvell's mother, and the attempts of Rumens' Marvell to maintain levity during a pandemic ('Your English, James, I find, /Keeps sweet the Latin essence, /Unspoiled by fancy dress-sense /Like Celia on my mind') will remind readers of more contemporary failures of tone and purpose under similar conditions.

Secretive though Marvell was, his appearance in Jon Thompson's 'In a Time of Floods' seems emblematic ('Andrew Marvell /I don't know why you're in this poem /unless it's because the coasts are now awash like the Humber in Hull'): a force of nature, welling up from mysterious sources and irrupting irresistibly. Born by 'the tide of Humber', Marvell's current of song is far-reaching and enduring. Haunting his green shade today, the poets gathered here can plausibly claim to number among Marvell's 'companions of my thoughts more green'.

Rotten Appleton

A white nun's ghost pursues Black Tom's
around the wreck of their old home,
a dead and standing pool of air;
here, Marvell wrote great poetry,
most copiously on this pile
All negligently overthrown,
off-limits too to living souls
by its new brewer-owner's rule,
a man stuck butt-deep in the past,
a puritan redux who banned
in his pubs music, mobile phones,
gay kisses, sportswear, motorbikes . . .
These Walls restrain the World without;
what he did gain he should maintain,
our landlord of this not-free house
so careless with his mansion old:
its grounds locked up, its roofs fall down,
its holy, militarised fields
from Marvell's poem, haunting still
where soldier and Cistercian join
in *gingling Chain-shot of her Beads*
ringed now by barbed-wire rosaries;
hermetic chain-link fencing weaves
a new quincuncial lozenge.
The owner of *this sober Frame*,
when floods destroyed the only bridge
where his home brewery is based,
refused the council leave to build
a pontoon from his unused land,
as this bridge to Marvell is lost
for his quadricentennial,
so I brew for the landlord here
(a man enraged by cursing too)

this curse I learned from Roman Bath:
sic liquat commodo aqua,
that he'll melt down to frothing wrath
(The river in itself is drowned)
on which floats snatches of Marvell
like splintered matchwood rafts that surf
iambic octosyllabics
rhyme's flooded bridge does not contain
around Nun Appleton, though banned,
being present quintessentially,
as living mouths leave mirrors moist
(let others tell the paradox).
Through moist reflections I reflect
on fallen arches with flat feet
from Leeds, a city back-to-front
and inside out and upside down,
according to the architect
who wrote a book about this town
which Black Tom won for Parliament,
but turned out since for royalty:
'The World Turned Upside Down', composed
while Marvell was still Royalist,
a song that once named many pubs
now mostly closed, as more will do:
Hospitality it selfe is drown'd.
The meaning for our landlord's clear:
although your inns do entertain
for now, they can't remain the same;
before Time's called on your trade wed
this heritage with industry,
take stock and take the time to read
your great house tenant's poetry,
a marvel ill-reflected here:
compare to my broad metaphors
his concentrated imagery,
devices self-inwoven fine
In Multiplying Glasses Lye,

a Neoplatonist conceit.
Compare his metre with this clock;
hear: *a green thought in a green shade:*
as natural as holding breath
before the beauty he evokes.
Compare these wet reflections with
his bone-dry wit and genius
at integrating opposites,
the circle in the quadrature
he makes a square grown spherical:
his art's *inverted Tree* is Klee's.
But what goes round comes round like rains
when skies inhale them back again,
so you might come around in time,
as Roundheads grew new curls in turn,
to love Marvell, my landlord friend,
then open to your house and heart
celestial society
and welcome people to these fields
that echo yet with Marvell's works,
for silent pages everywhere
are louder than artillery.
We'll both pass soon to the Abyss:
you could take poets' blessings there,
there is still time, though I can hear
its wingèd drayhorse drawing close,
iambic hoofbeats that may break
the peace you built from emptiness
annihilating all you've made
inside your fine and private place.
The iron gates you've raised won't keep
the elements or winds at bay,
nor you or I from thirsty ground;
therefore, before we've hell to pay,
allow Marvell's Fifth Element
to mist new glasses at our lips:
I'll buy the drinks; let's sing this round.

Dents-de-Lion

for Jane

For Marvell's four hundredth anniversary,
and our fortieth, driving to Nun Appleton
we'd find our world locked out, the estate
invested in ruination by some new owner.

Coming back, we turned at a gate opening
onto a field plush with dandelions in seed,
old Belisha beacons losing their white hair.
We stopped to see clocks shower soft tufts

into May air and birdsong, blowing over
iron gates and chain-link fencing to leave
pads on stalks like buttons on green foils.

Sweetness, let us hold each other and roll
in our quilt until it bursts like a blowball,
while we may, while our own roads allow.

Triptych

i: The Buds Have Grown Restrained

First, every twig & bud seemed new;
today, the wood is decaying,
the high branches crumbling.

We are not their companions, we
do not think in the presence of them.

Our flesh is heavy, our bodies loose.

This outpouring of breaths has killed the ratio of hellos; we are more
disappeared — do not say a little;
this is the ugliness we had seen,
        rotting indoors. And here are the plants now,
        and here the roads,
here the daffodils, & all the flowers
whose names I try to know.

ii: Things Without Tongues

but the buds the buds!   how can you hear the buds silently
waiting to make spring
how can I-t

cause you to hear
the bark of the tree
not the flutter of birds' wings
you cannot hear that

       do not claim space by sound

birds   no!
      buds
can you hear them
through your skin that covers the earth
      ?
can you hear them through voice disappearing
      ?
is what remains
   thing & thing & thing
      ?
meaning buds meaning bark meaning grass
      meaning   their sound –
      meaning
      not
        the sound of birds!

the far limbs of the ancestor
have bonded with the sapling's brain,
the old tree has opened gate water.
they're joined where the scar of new skins
wrap themselves slowly round each other.
I only see them now because
of the dying of the light, the
leaves' slow death returning,
inches of skin connecting.

Two Hillsides

after Marvell, 'Epigramma in Duos Montes'

Two wild heights make the valley – Wharmton Hill
and a bleaker outcrop known locally
as Pots and Pans, old glacial rubble, dark,
flanked by low farms. Beyond the scarp, a war

memorial keeps straining like the neck
of Atlas taking credit for the sky.
Legend has it wet craters in the rocks
(and hence the name) can cure the eye of blights.

I never found that. Looking further east
to Wharmton's sunlit, green-baize flirt of treeline,
I can't help noticing the quarry there –
stoic, undaunted, emptied, quieted.

Its fleeting dance keeps changing. I can't help
but stare at it, help think: something once made
these two flung looming contraries collide,
these two perfected distances.

The Pennines keep returning in my mind,
breaking the light up with their roughened stride.
I think of the wrecks of mills and factories,
their children coughing fibres at the sun.

Trudge of the singing fathers, drunk, crept home
in darkness once; the valley kept around them.
Twin darknesses contending for the heights –
two sides. Dark stones dilating like a vision.

'Tis Marvellous Strange

We drain the fen to make our children's wars,
lack time enough and world to put it right
but cloak our woes in double-dealing cause

This time enough and world becomes our lore
when time-enough slips slowly out of sight
yet, still, we leech the land of oil and ore.

Apologists are quick to speak up for
the trickle-down effect of monied might
that rescues then exploits the fabled poor,

maintaining them to fight their profit wars.
As time enough and world gets ever tight
the middle look to guard their children's cause

and double-spoken pieties perform
to strategize and guard their subtle rights.
The rich man knows right well what tax is for:

avoiding it is nine-tenths of his law.
Your coyness then is surely now a flaw
sans time enough and world to make it right.
Let's use what's left to ransom and restore.

Cormack's quarry

> 'Heavens King
> Keeps register of every thing:
> And nothing may we use in vain.'
> — Marvell, *'The Nymph Complaining of the Death of Her Faun'*

1.

The plants are quiet as I cross generations
of grass. A fly dies on my coat, leaves guts,
a sheen of yellow wing. Mist balances the hills.
We're machinery with our breathing
and swallowing, our opening and closing
of gullet, urethra. The slippery tang of cheese,
streak of water in throat. Now I'm alone, will I hear
them singing, the fuchsias, heather with its pink
flowers budding, fat-stubbed clover in purple
and cream, cocks and hens. They have so much
to tell, these water avens, soldiers and the grasses
that cover their stems with glowing leaf, crowns
with bud or spikelet, this damp-loving sedge
grown over rock in layer and ridge, blade and tuft.

2.

I'm knee-deep, unable to twist.
This used to be water, I once tried to sail it
with a friend on a makeshift raft.
It's a living thing – not quite cold –
lugging at my legs, making me bend
from the waist, drop my signalless phone
into a gloop that's caking my hands
and hair, a landlubber biped in the house
of the mud hogboon. Every human

in the world, invisible imprint with a backpack
of bread and cheese, here without offering
to the hill's hollowed-out places. The wells
I make close back with a thick sucking;
I walk the mud floor in my socks.

3.

Do you feel water in you when the rain falls?
Your composite casing collapses inwards,
dissolution of bone and skin, sluicing into
your earth-well womb, centering upwards,
lungs and cerebrum descending? Slocked emotion,
surrendered soul, reliquary of cell and spittle,
sickness and synapse caving into a collective.
The mix of earth and water pulls me,
plants feet into rock that will move against rock
while stars gestate. Just as the unfluffed mill
of my mind is plexal, so is this floor elastic;
it leads to liquid, between which the centre
of a celestial thing. My mind scarps the surface
in ligament to its stone embryos.

The Blower Against Gardens

Between this man's feet and the levelled earth
lay a carpet of plastic turf
on beds of polypropylene and sand,
concrete mixed and screeded by hand.
He planned and failed to fell the witch's tree;
a rowan ripe with scarlet berries.
Dug up the bunch of tulips and the rose
but underneath his bulbous nose,
dormant roots and knotweed's dogged rhizomes
spun and stretched and searched like genomes.
In borders he cut blue-grey limestone and wedged
bulk slate chippings up to the edge,
lined the paths with rock-shaped solar lights
pointing the way into the night.
One afternoon he browsed the whole world through
to find his hot tub at *B&Q*,
ordered a fire pit and garden bench,
charcoal stain for shed and fence.
With pallets and plywood he built a cocktail bar
in the garage by his car,
toasted a job well done with his only vice:
rhubarb gin with tonic and ice.
Weekly he vacuums the lawn till bare and clean,
scrubs the pavers so each fleck gleams,
and when the leaves and rowanberries fall
he starts his blower and eats them all.
As for the weeds that find routes to push up,
he spikes their leaves with spritz of *Roundup*.
One last sweep before his guest arrives;
errant twigs he can't abide
he'll use to stoke the fire whenever it's dwindling
then snap in two to use for kindling.

Like the flower that yields and blooms at four,
he opens the bar by remote control door,
invites you in to drink your health by the pyre,
talks of heights to which he aspires.
And while the blackened hulks of last logs glow
as tumours blossom and cancers grow,
his day will temper and chase its natural end,
and this plot of his is yours to tend.

blue air

the estuary shining

a deer on wasteland
beyond the end of the path

a winter's day walk

breaking the ice on a puddle
doesn't break my concentration

i'm at the edge of the world

enjoying the noise from the refinery

steam escaping into the blue air

i'm not afraid of failure
not afraid of getting old

reeds at the edge of the river
set my thoughts in motion
in the opposite direction to language

at my approach the deer looks up

it runs off
and i know i can't follow

i'm not afraid to get lost

A Few More Years in Residence

It's not only that summer's done,
but that his light has fallen and the garden
looks awry with all reason gone.

The Humber rolls to its new owner's
rule, and he'll not know how
or why his city drowned.

And when the following years go to bed
he'll be left in his peace with time
served in subservience to grief.

It's all this place has shown, tempestuous winds
and a new world for those unencumbered
by the reason for all of his questions.

English Pastoral

> *My vegetable love should grow*
> *Vaster than empires, and more slow*
> — Marvell

–unseasonable storm's
mustered
axe of air

Wood powdering,
brittle as
ancestral lace

Gored in its core-stump
a rusted
spike

Hung-out bare
like a cuspid tooth
in a carious mouth

Time crept centuries
circling
an iron I

I
stroke it, lightly:
my diabolic amulet

A tree's corralled vigil:
the abrupt
amputee's fate.

I can't cull
your orphaned
shadows

The green
hallucinations
of history are still yours to reap –

The Wandering Statues of Marvell and Larkin

Parla, parla, ascoltando ti sto! [Speak, speak, I am listening to you!] –
— Don Giovanni to the Stone Guest

I stand outside my grammar school and Holy Trinity. My father,
Master of the Charterhouse and lecturer at this same Holy Trinity,
Drowned, sand-warpt in the Humber, together with the drunken boatmen,
Coming home. And so I left my other fenland Trinity for France and Italy.

I stand amongst the throng at Paragon, for all the world as though I'm late
Getting away. My father, City Treasurer, left unhindered from a dingy ward,
From cancer. At 63. Like me. And so I left for Belfast, after Leicester,
To more books. Eventually, and finally, to here. I hate abroad.

I fled my King and country in the war and came back to the Grove at Bill-borow.
Here in the Garden of the World, this Paradise, I praised the magick of the green,
To discourse with the breathing trees, the holy mathematicks of Nun Appleton.
Shady forests, grassy meadows like green silk, this Nursery of all things green,

Green thought in a green shade, the mower's song, in the greenness
Of the grass, seeing hopes as in a glass, and death, who is a mower too.
And then assistant to the Commonwealth, to Milton and to Parliament, to King,
And businessmen in Hull with bribes and licences. To all the green, adieu.

Oh, I missed the war. Half blind, you see. And I tried twice to get into
The Civil Service, but they never wanted me. But I could see the trees
In Pearson Park and Hessle and the Cemetery. Work. The books and girls
Inside the flattened cube of light. And Betjeman and Amis. Holderness. The sea.

Fenced and unfenced. Bicycles, tombs. The everyday. Elegiac to demotic
And back again, they say. Always the jazz, at least, despite the conferences
And papers. And cut grass, and the mower and the hedgehog. Trees. Bloody toads
And bridges. And finally, those scruffy porters, propitiatory flowers, absences…

Oh, come with me! I've been around the town, in City Hall, and Bond Street,
Savile Street and George Street, where my arse was blackened in the Blitz.
Latterly, in front of William Gee. But now I'm here. Let's go and see King Billy
Or Victoria, Wilberforce, or de la Pole, *or talk to that green man showing his bits,*

And ask him why he's called Voyage, for God's sake, and why he's facing south
When he's supposed to be on the lookout for his mate in Iceland. Or test our wits
Penning new lines about coy mistresses and graves here by the Humber's Mouth.
Though, like yesterday, we seem dead, just stone and bronze, not living flesh, it's
Clear we're here. Begin afresh our green conceits. Something always to be said.

Hibari

> *The World when first created sure*
> *Was such a Table rase and pure.*
> — 'Upon Appleton House

I

In dreams of Eden an old lark lives
Proffering a breast to every horny theist.
Watch one suck two nails into her gullet:
Her tongue comes away with a nick.
 Later that sleeping theist dreams
A nascent rail, drowning, slithering
In the Trevi, buoyed by a circlet of copper
Penny wishes, sopping with holy dew.
What music in Eden, and by God, what sin!

II

Past avenues of tar, gullies thick with smog,
His ever-vacant house, in its ever-vacant spot.
You know its capsized ceiling: a fishing rod
Jammed into one side: the chimney a bamboo
Minaret, capped with a copy of his horseshoe
Hand cast from that first time he dared
To cradle the bloodless Earth, score
His fingertips on her topography.
 And here every bird will sleep.

III

Marvel how the mowed rail
Rose with a jaw in one clutch,
Its open heart in the other,
And still hiccupped its song.
 How could it stand
The splayed crest her leaking,
The wound's white-lipped pucker,
Stand the morning air so brackish,
Sterilised by Eden's dew water?

IV
The rail fled to a pebble-beach peninsula
Where she, the lark, and the wren
Mothers sang a song of communes.
In crooked cathedrals of silver
Birch twigs, their frozen eggs. Rearing
Each other's winter hatchlings, they mourned
The yolk of one hundred failed kingdoms.
   O Lord, tell me a truth in exchange
For a poem: was there bigotry among the birds?

Anniversary

Chinese lanterns! Their dull lights
a dotted line across the dark
that pulsed and dipped and lost its flight
piece by piece, in Belton Park.

You caught a shooting star, and poked
at where it was. Too late. We sat
in different chairs, ineffably yoked,
sipping wine, and watched a bat

wheel out and back, while glow-worms pulsed
between the logs, and grasses frisked.
Perfect. You didn't want anything else.
I wasn't ready to take the risk.

Dialogue between the Body and the Brain

BODY
Is body's suit still present, tense,
detained in nonsense by each sense?
Broken by bones, stressed by these feet,
handcuffed by hands, eaten by meat;
put on the blink by eyes, and by
hearing unaided where tongues tie;
alive with wires and charged with crimes,
atomic, clocked by troubled times,
in shares and parts falling apart;
still beaten by both brow and heart?

BRAIN
And only body's voiced by voice.
Accent's accented by thyroids
and words are worded by the past,
by some old bodies' type and cast.
Perhaps thought fills up so much room
because it's just a frilled mushroom
neuming through us its chantarelle . . .
Would tortoises wear humanshell
had they instead been made its host?
Would they too call it Holy Ghost?

BODY

How can this to those heights aspire
when respiration will expire,
breathing, pneumatic as a drill,
stop deep? And this is not a drill;
nothing's as selfish as our selves'
(what Huxley called) reducing valves,
maintaining every streaming brain's
more orifices than a train,
training its means towards some end
wherein's no meaning to prehend.

BRAIN

Are doctored doctors, then, a joke
versus the pain loose ends provoke?
Those show: time's tabled to be turned
and buttons panic, suns are burned
and insecure attachments leak,
not finding what, hiding, they seek.
Gloria mundi's made mundane,
is coloured by this human stain
whose senses can't be reconciled,
since every adult hoods its child,
pretends to knowledge, never knows
why we pretend no-shows are shows.
The mystery lies there –
as evident as video; as square.

Appleton Revisited

after Andrew Marvell

1

But grasshoppers are giants there.

Ocean of meadow,
its waves breached by grasshoppers –
dry leviathans.

Whalesong squeaks out of the depths,
78 rpm.

Sunken gold kingcups,
coral reefs of campion.
Periwinkles squirm.

Waves cloven by the strimmer's
eardrum-rupturing jetski.

Lifejacket whistle
sounding mayday from the blue:
a lark cast adrift.

Flotsam of nettle and stalk
where the Atlantic was wrecked.

2

It seems indeed as Wood not Trees.

In the wood's darkness
I have shut myself away –
chesspiece in a box.

Caught in the footpath's clutches
I'm circumscribed by brambles.

Exam-hall stillness.
My invigilating steps.
Woodpecker ticking.

Drone of a solitary bee,
a thought keeping its distance.

Glimpses through the slats
of the wood's vertical blind.
It's raining out there,

a million fingers tapping
on my million umbrellas.

In the Garden

The summer was huge, and hugely gone.
Then woke to racketing communion;
hedge to hedge in sudden loud return.

Spectrum-sparked starlings
interrupting elsewhere's urgent song.
That big low sun still bumping along.

At your feet, a froglet's quick flick.
Sunning on the lily-pad,
old Bloat-King clears his throat.

No plop into a Basho haiku,
just stares you out
as late damsonfly jidder jade.

Wind-falls. Cloud-race. Shade.
Everything glows.
Falls. Fades.

Sometime this week, check
if there's still some life left
in your old winter coat. Dig it out.

Your shadow boxes with you as you pass,
already long across the freshened grass.
And it's all grass. All long sheaved grass.

Lanterns

"Carnation, Lily, Lily, Rose" 1885-86,
John Singer Sargent, Tate Britain, London

"... at a certain notation of the light [he] ran forward over the lawn with the action of a wag-tail, planting at the same time rapid dabs of paint on the picture, and then retiring again, only with equal suddenness to repeat the wag-tail action. All this occupied but two or three minutes, the light rapidly declining, and then while he left the young ladies to remove his machinery, Sargent would join us again, so long as the twilight permitted, in a last turn at lawn tennis."

— *Edmund Gosse, letter to Evan Carteris.*

1.

There's a painting I like to remember
from the museum of my childhood:
a Victorian garden on a summer evening
 – quietly vibrant, rich-hued, pigment more vivid
by the glowing screen than my mind's eye blur.

Two young girls in lambent smocks
light paper lanterns in a flower-thick corner.
They've set others, orange-pink, to hang
behind the lilies' heavy-headed droop,
big globes and drums all spilling light.

It stops there, caught in that twilit moment,
as the lanterns flush rose on nape and cheek,
highlight frills on lilies, dresses' edging,
bronze threads burning through the hair
the painter wants to catch just so.

Who knows what happens next?
Will they hoist those lanterns high on poles
so that swinging glow now slows,
pauses bright as it turns, then dips to waltz
through the mauve harmonics of the dusk?

2.

Sargent has no time for what comes next;
he is there to catch what's already gone.
Over the weeks, earlier and earlier,
he keeps his appointment with the light
– dwindling minutes to make it live again.

Each evening, he dashes out,
into the fleeting summer;
worries canvas, those fine adjustments,
stipples paint to get that light just right.

Come September, he's out dead-heading.
Come October, showers and shivers,
some days he doesn't get to paint,

or he's hanging paper-tissue flowers,
lanterns lit earlier and earlier,

against the coming night.

Glow-Worms

lampyris noctiluca

1.

These *living lamps* now all but doused;
country comets fizzled in childhood's ditch.

All quite put out tonight, those foolish fires;
the way our childhood's memories
of other childhoods glimpsed in books
went the way of sticklebacks,
daddy-longlegs, or the grass snake caught
skipping through the zero of itself:
now you see it, now it's gone.

Summer's eve, *the courteous lights* withdraw.
The path by dawn seems clear, though bleak,
much emptier than it seemed by night.

2.

And Tommy in the muddy trench,
for the umpteenth time since the orders came,
reading his sweetheart's careful cursive,
folds worn through her Lady's vellum,
sealed with a kiss and stolen scent
by the jam-jar of cold green light.

3.

Poor beetle,
misunderstood, misnamed.
Can't fly these broken bounds,
hedged in by roads,
you must sit and wait it out,
turn your wingless body into light.

4.

Flightless, under a sliver of moon,
kindling herself into ever sharper green
that's lit with the eeriness of life.

Nightly, in the dusky haze,
her beacon burns a morse pinpoint
until a male drops by, is doused.

Eggs laid,
a day or two before she also fades,
all the light of her life
quite put out.

The Marvellous Garden

> *And yet these rarities might be allowed*
> > *To man, that sovereign thing and proud,*
> *Had he not dealt between the bark and tree,*
> > *Forbidden mixtures there to see.*
> *No plant now knew the stock from which it came;*
> > *He grafts upon the wild the tame*
> *That the uncertain and adulterate fruit*
> > *Might put the pate in dispute.*
> > > — 'The Mower against Gardens'

If Man was made in the spit and image of God
> then He Himself looks pretty odd.
Ditto the creatures Man has proudly bred
> (the wilder ones he leaves for dead)
– experiments which cast, sooner or later,
> harsh light on their manipulator.
And so our freaks of nature, deformed, unfit,
> reveal a human Identikit
in whose dark mirror meddling Man may see
> his road to Eschatology.

As Man's best friend down from the cuddly surface
> has been rejigged, improved, repurposed,
with crippled hips, short breath and weakened jaw,
> docked tail, flopped ears and clawless paw,
so, as well as Fauna, the Flora too
> is re-created, made brand-new.
Our trek from Genesis to Revelation,
> now passes through these vast plantations
where patented monocultured GM crops
> lay waste the forest and ancient copse.

The farmer's sold the farm, it's all Big Pharma,
> unnatural selection's the modern karma,
whereby we get not what we think we sow,
> but what the Petri dish can grow:
new genes from ancient double helix strands
> untwisted by technicians' hands.
Was Eden really full of harmless beasts?
> That's what the Bible claims at least.
Was our persuasive friend, the talking snake,
> the only predator on the make?

In the Peaceable Kingdom, before it all got damned,
> did Lion cuddle up to Lamb?
That Pre-Lapsarian garden seems so twee,
> with thornless rose and stingless bee;
none of all that red in tooth and claw
> but wagging tails, soft padded paw.
No savagery, no violence or disease,
> mosquitos, tarantulas or fleas.
Vegan lions, bears and crocodiles,
> no need for camouflage or guile.

That life in Eden seemed so very dull
> never enter God's great skull?
The *Garden* may be a kind of metaphor,
> but, still, He never quite foresaw
the way his puny playthings like to play,
> inventing stuff to pass the day.
Homo Sapiens isn't quite so dim
> –but likes to make things, just like Him.
Man can't leave Nature well enough alone:
> DIY's bred in his bone.

For in his mind Man is a kind of god
        conjuring miracles from the sod.
He has a passion for the strange and new:
        Let science break through old taboos!
And now he's mixing up those disparate genes,
        reading data off the screens.
It seems the latest figures from in the field
        predict a grossly increased yield.
It's working well, if you believe your eyes;
        the crops shoot up, share prices rise.

Halal, haram, the lawful and the forbidden,
        what's for the table, what's for the midden;
Leviticus and Deuteronomy
        likewise list what's best left be.
Now nothing's kosher, nothing's kept apart;
        a pig inherits a gorilla's heart.
Though neither fish nor fowl, not bug nor plant,
        crops spliced with cells from lizard, ant
may soon go hopping down the future's road
        with DNA from frog or toad.

Back then, those tulips with the most prized streaks
        were not the fittest but the freaks:
those patterns caused by viruses, disease,
        drove tulipmania's strange bêtise.
Now Man is searching for the Holy Grail,
        through mixing up new gene cocktails.
Miscegenation is his strategy,
        as he twists and bends biology
to a Boschian monster mash-up, half-beast, half-flora,
        – the mutton tree, the flowering fauna.

Man went forth and multiplied: still more
> strange hybrid creatures, sports galore,
then slowly, distracted by the new and weird,
> noticed how much had disappeared.
The garden, once abundant and diverse,
> now seemed less marvellous than cursed.
So much had gone from his Edenic plot:
> elephants, tigers, almost the lot
had dwindled one by one down through the ages
> to connoisseur specimens kept in cages.

Birds and insects, frogs and fruits and flowers
> near vanquished by Man's god-like powers,
while all around this poor, diminished scene
> rose uniform regiments of genes:
vast horizons of monocultured zones
> tended by robotic clones.
Things were getting samey, but also weird.
> Some odd new hybrids now appeared.
Miscegenation reached another level,
> as Man now rivalled both god and devil.

Eg, the latest thing in crop rotation:
> these plants exceeding their lowly station,
uproot themselves, grow legs to cross the lands
> to silos where with dexterous hands
they harvest themselves before their fruit can spoil.
> They then return, re-root in soil.
That at least was Man's so cunning plan,
> before the shit had hit the fan.
No longer planted, they go marauding free,
> like Triffids on a killing spree.

Weird Venus fly-traps, they've learned to feed on flesh
    – dogs and cats, they like them fresh.
The Garden's a nightmare, what was tame's now wild:
    see flower-beds slurp up a child.
The future's out of control. Out of Man's hands.
    God knows, he was always truly damned
to live by brain and brawn, the sweat of his brow.
    So still, so just as then so now,
beyond the Garden forged with his own two hands.
    still stretch the low and level sands.

Train to Cambridge

These British fields straight out
of British poetry, bucolic green
and stunningly mediocre, except

when—and in one exceptional
case—the green becomes long
fields of yellow flowers, postmodern

and ultra-lemony, quite wrong
against the greyish cloudy sky,
yet also very right like the essential

tension in all good to great British
poetry, that of what's not British
at its center, the transplanted element,

the other, the elsewhere intrinsic
but tokenised or most times
unacknowledged. I can't remember

such a green in most bucolic
British poems, but then, on occasion,
as in Clare, because of his odd,

jaunty eye for observation, my eye
feels instantly sympathy as one
shape, and so the other, myself,

is there as a given. The train stops.
Beyond the platform, so close,
is a typical redbrick house, the window

draped with white curtains, fresh
from the 19th century!, so causal,
so blighty, so much the husk

of a poem, a house often presumed
to be quiet and orderly, yet the lemony
shock of green which lives on the edge

that is poetry, the other, is there.
Marvell's poetry for instance.
Restoration Marvell, overseeing

the ruins renewed at Court
like a coifed Nehemiah. Still, his volte-face
betrays no idle insight, praising

England's supreme gardener, Milton:
"much gravity and ease." And I, star-led
in my sixth form glossed to memory:

"the *Common wealth* doth by its losses grow,"
stowed for some future malice—
which time has come. Off again.

More meadows. A few sunken ponds.
Marvell is gone, and you, I see you
gathering those lemony flowers

from the fields of some time back,
grandmother, great armfuls spilling
behind you, but you don't mind,

moving with stealth through purging
flax staining your knees—and here again,
the train draws right into my eyes

another of those great lemon fields,
then stops. The station is Elsenham.
At that moment, a bird's uncontrollable

cry breaks out, my own sudden *cahier
d'un retour au pays natal* slams bright
with your yellow flowers in my chest.

A New English Translation of an Epistle by Andrew Marvell

Honoured Doctor Witty,
Your rendering of this Thesis
On Quacksalves (unlike Chris's)
Reminds me of my pretty

Celia – Marvellous Girl
Who slips through tongues like Tagus -
Or the myrrh-bearing magus -
Through Spain and Portugal.

Your English, James, I find,
Keeps sweet the Latin essence,
Unspoiled by fancy dress-sense
Like Celia on my mind.

Ah! Though she babbles French
So freely, her complexion
and lips, beyond correction,
declare a blushing wench

from 'Ull. Ooh eck, I've strayed,
in feverish peroration,
again, from your translation…
How truly, Sir, you've said

That, worst of all abuses
In Pharmaceuticals -
Worse than Saints' Cuticles
Or Transubstantial Juices -

Is Woman as Physician.
It can't be stressed too often
For any man who's coughin'
That Celia's disposition

Within Galenic Science
Is among broths and cawdles,
To weep when the egg curdles
Or the invalid expires.

*Marvell's poem (written in English) is addressed "To his worthy Friend Doctor Witty *upon his Translation of the Popular Errours". The latter was a collection of medical fallacies. Marvell's address to James Witty focuses on the art of translation, but includes some misogynist asides. It's possible that the entire poem is meant ironically.*

The Grass to the Mower

The Israeli militia call their operations in Gaza 'mowing the grass'

You allowed us a patch of dirt
outside your garden-city
but, as you dug towards us,
 you saw we were too close, so close
your scythes lit up the night.
Eviction-therapy.
Mowing-therapy.
Topiary of non-negotiation.

Our fury dissipated,
tracers thinning on the iron dome
above your iron garden,
your spreading Scythedom.
But you cried out your people were mown down
because you hadn't mown us off the earth.

We're straw, we're smoke
outside your garden city.
Inside your garden-city, too,
there's withering and crying.
 A mania of mowing hits the lands,
the tiniest grass-blades learning how to mow
in schools of desolation.
Holocaust-restoration.
Desert-defloration.

The grass is scything, scything.

(May 18th, 2021)

The Mower Redux

Like this tree. Buried under herbs
& flowers. Purity disturbs

it. Fungus eating through the small
leaves. Tiny cankers. A shortfall

in vigor meeting the desire
to fail. But in failed speech a higher

order sticks. True survey. & in
green gardens green annihilation

speaks. You are a dream baby caught
in wool. The enemy of thought

is thinking. Problems talk away
themselves in time. As hay binds hay.

As love is subjects, endlessly
combined. Inflected. Like this tree.

Dying leaves a perfume

after Andrew Marvell

she loves to die
in the green grass

in transparent floods
so straight and green

on a small boat
in all the meadows

I have known
stand still shadows

gather the flowers
hours clouds a leaf

a fever recollecting
its own light the

winds listening
strange and high

The Rose-Giver

The one lady owner of all you see,
Receive a further rose from me,
Bearing carefully in mind
This latest bloom must also serve
As notice that I have resigned.

It would be foolish to suppose
That there will always be a rose
To flatter your imperious whim.
The lover and the lowest slave
Must seek their pleasures in the grave.

If from that grave – as no one knows -
There should uncoil a pure black rose,
The shade of your unnatural heart
And outcome of unnatural art,
Best not to wish for one of those.

An Insurrection

Airborne gods of an imagined purity
promised to deliver an outsized victory
by hot miracles of flint strike and spark,
a saturnalian flutter by lodestar and shark
or burning flags; a steady accumulation of money
along with banknotes candied in honey.

No matter about the usual connections and security:
this new culture of entitlement and tomfoolery
went unnoticed as the flutter of curtains in an empty room
in the metropole from whose citadel a boom
was highly likely. Months of suspicion and conspiracy
went unchecked by the gatekeepers of democracy.

Gods whose varieties of moonscapes and palaces
owed their glow and ferocity to credit advances.
Yet their chief aim in this city was protecting ornamental
talismans while their rituals of light and hope found a portal
for violence, and recalling those leopards who broke
(despite all desperate beliefs this was a joke)
into the temple in Kafka's fable of sacrifice,
leave it for us to declare, at least, that it will suffice
that special instructions remain necessary:
the rebels would be incorporated into the ceremony.

The Garden

    an ecopoetic version of Gavin Douglas, *'Palice of Honour'*, (c. 1540).

I was doing my qi-
  gong in the walled garden
    bathed in sun
scorchio as heaven
  among criss-cross
    branches pixililtated
with blossom

sad-face Dawn
  had wrapped
    her cosy rosy robes
round the soft-beds
  of the flower-lass
    May

She's stitched
  her flowery blanket
    with shiny gems –
ruby, topaz, pearl
  & emerald

petals dew-
  dropped   the fresh
    & fragrant air
breathed in
  a verdant shimmer
    along the paths
breathed out a haze
  that hung in the
    woods

in their niches
  aromatic flowers
    spread beneath
a matrix of leaves
  suffused with
    the divine harmonies
of birds perched
  on twigs & branches
    each adding a
sweet song to the din
  of notes that echo
    off buds & boughs
and reverberated
  to the skies

while I daunered
  in this idyll
    full of the joys
out of The Firth
  I saw The Sun
    come driving
over the waves
  like a yellow camper
    van replete
with gold hub-caps
  and a freshly
    painted bonnet
      that gleamed so

birds, flowers, trees
  they all felt great
    to see Sol
looking so hip

the daisies & marigolds
  unfurled for there's
    no more need
to curl their leaves
  in the dark
    fending off dank
air and toxic
  mould

on the skyline
  Gaia's shady woodland
    stood in silhouette
revived by the life-
  giving rays whose
    warmth is
so energizing

this time of year
  everything flourishes
    grasshoppers nip
at the grass
  bees mend
    the hive

winds disappear
  frosts scarper
    bad omens are
out on their arse

Sun is shining
  its beams cheer
    each wee thing
that's growing

I listened to the
  stream pattering be-
    tween its grassy banks

the entire ecotone
  tenderly verdant
    exuding heat

the earth glinting
  with ores and quartz

I felt comfort and joy
  but in my reverie
    I wasn't sure
was this lovely
  garden reality
    or fantasy?

wandering among
  the shrubbery
    I heard a voice
as bright as the sun
  call out:

"May, mirror of souls
  Month of the Earth
    and muse

 your generosity
  and wildcraft
    boosts the wee herbs

your biotic progress
  is remedy and remediation
    causing the fruits
to produce
you dispense grace
  on every living thing."

By the tide of Humber
    (In 1641 Andrew Marvell's father was drowned crossing the Humber in a barrow boat. The poet's 'To his Coy Mistress' *was written some nine years later.)*

    Which way to walk? eastwards by ebbtide,
    past the stink of the upriver staiths
    and a small brick school between garden and church,
    to the spit of Spurn, that land's-end shifter,

    or westwards inland, the estuary shrinking
    till you'd almost walk across sandbanks and mud
    southwards to Cambridge—the way out, straight
    by Ermine Street, for a Roman departure.

    Now, *I by the tide of Humber* once more
    ponder these shallows more lethal than deeps,
    and a barrow boat, grounded, where a wash of water
    unpicks what was lost of him bit by bit—

    and think, no *fine or private place*
    was his, just the city's effluent waste
    seeping seawards, the spirit of him held
    forever in the tide's endless erasures,

    till Spurn divides sea-lippers from the still,
    to curb the hackling flow that pours
    salt into fresh, daily, and seems
    a hurt refreshed, a trouble restored.

    Now I, by the tide, still whisper farewells.
    Te patre, Caesar[1] (royal head or round?)--
    my warring self by such waters crossed:
    fluvial, marine, knitting frets between,

---

1 'you father, Caesar', from Marvell's earliest known student poem in Latin, published in Cambridge, 1637.

where contrary currents make shifting sands
channel a rip-tide, then swing and suck
any light craft under—as if I carry
his death within, unfinished, unsung.

So I, by the waters that quarrel and kill,
stay, for contraries no war resolves,
to complain of love in verse that hides
an elegy, deep in the undertow of *tide*.

Short Song for Andrew Marvell

Andrew Marvell, who knows about your speck
of consciousness four hundred years ago
amidst a far-off island's rushed tableaux
of kings and lost republics? You also speak

in deft erasures of yourself, evading
our eyes more quickly than we can forget you –
you change your costume, get rid of your goatee,
take ship or don't, cross-hatch the portrait's shading,

turn meadows mowed down into massacres,
then turn these into seething ocean floors,
then constellations, mirrors, canvasses,

a face (your own?) that talks with different voices,
before you magick it back into acres
of broad and silent pasture, wind through flowers.

The Garden

> *Fair trees! wheres'e'er your barks I wound,*
> *No name shall but your own be found.*

1.

Out of the sheath dress
gently hopping, sparrow in the lot below
in the great complacency of summer
pressing down, waves of it
what can the plants do but endure this closeness
the trees, their varieties, and ivy, nameless shrubs
and hedges, no one speaks their names
only flowers get that nod and certain grasses
so that when a day of cooler breath in July
airs out the neighborhood you feel
for a moment the rustling in lindens, oaks, sycamores
as they sense what's been withheld
for months, that's when the mature ones
rustle it off, slip almost
sexily out of that dress, unbearable
to feel such potential against one's skin

2.

Out in the open trees behave differently.
They stand differently, their posture is different.
They might look at you
if that held any interest.
They really dare live alongside,
coexist. Their enormity
which doesn't need your lifted gaze
has time in it. Where we live, planted
in the span between sidewalk and street
they play their part with competence
and often commitment, invested.
They're good at being trees.

3.

Tall ones
this airport weather, an April
processing this way from which
direction I can't tell, for you is
individual, like dollars owed or
today's shirt
you stand looking gently
down shaking heads
preparing us, your very slow branches saying little

Emerging Moth

and studying all the summer night

First the living lamps
above me went
awry, then I felt a sky
inside myself, a need
for infinite retreat.
Revenge is sweet,
but charity is sweeter.
All my chlorophyll
nibbles have come
to this. Left to my own
advice, I would have cruised
the piney underbrush
in search of future lust,
anticipating every
moony, dim
chromatic scale.
Instead I will
set sail: my still-
inflating flowing
wings, hesitatingly
spread, are open doors
to a littler generation,
to safety for my genes
and shelter for my next
of kin, my place in
the world to come. I did
what I came here to do. I will
never see the sun.

In a Time of Floods

Still water under a still sky
        the old landscape has disappeared
and the old languages are dying
        Andrew Marvell
I don't know why you're in this poem
        unless it's because the coasts
are now awash like the Humber in Hull
        floods again are drowning streets and houses
two-hundred year floods tolling every two years
        so much swept up and away by water and wind
in the aftermath lost signs are lost promises
        what are the words that'll summon the new world
we need to want
        I'm afraid we won't come up with the right words
I'm afraid that even if we do it's
        too late
in the aftermath waters that were roiling and enraged
        have reached a point
of perfect equipoise of
        irrefutable glassiness
everything that was simply *there*
        everything that was a given
is now a backwards-running story
        running toward the silence of water
O singer of the garden
        we need the words to again
be that bright and new

The Glow-Worm to the Mower

Since you're unlikely to astound
yourself by having more to save
than hay, small wonder you've not found
why wave upon successive wave

would summon, far inland, sea-sounds
from a dull scythe or sickle.
When Juliana and you downed
tools to lunch on cheese and pickles

atop the triangular mound
with its outcrop of hairy vetch
for which your meadow is renowned
it must have felt like the home stretch

to a safe harbor. Black horehound
in the sheugh... The sun a sea-gong...
All afternoon you would expound
on how a mower must be strong

while Juliana, tightly wound
as ever, slowly went off-script,
the vetch-garland with which she's crowned
having by dusk completely slipped,

the ties by which lovers are bound
also substantially weakened.
We mourn all those poor souls who've drowned
because our own inconstant beacons

have led to their running aground;
bear in mind it's by, and from, you
(and not the other way around)
we glowworms steer and take our cue.

In search of Appleton

When Marvell was tutor at Nun Appleton he would have attended the local church of All Saints, Bolton Percy.

Within this sober frame expect
Lines short, words fit, and circumspect.
The scene, a church, that swells with pride
For he who once set foot inside.
Not sacred Fairfax, no, nor Vere
Had brought us, pilgrims, to worship here.
The name that caused these walls to swell
Was the poet's name, Andrew Marvell!

Why in his poem had Marvell not,
Discoursed upon this sacred spot?
A religious house, yet how
So unremarked upon, 'til now?
A church devoted to All Saints,
But left untouched by he who paints
The liveliest woods and rural scene,
A Lely of words and thoughts more green.

When Marvell invites us to round
Our pleasant footsteps on this ground,
Past ruins and swelling halls we run
Past pieties ended, and new begun,
But opts he always to conceal
That church which we today reveal,
As though a secret, last and best,
A treasure trove and treasure chest.

A place where Marvell lived and breathed!
Where heard he Henry Fairfax read
The Sunday sermon. Here reposed,
Was this where he his poem composed?
His admirable lines? And can I, too,
Find inspiration in this wooden pew?
Can I feel my way back, mayhap,
To paradise's only map?

True, paradise is but a page
And Marvell's but a long-lost age,
Where kings were killed and battles fought,
And mowers kept the grasses short.
Now tractors plough the levelled ground,
And barbed wire fences fields around.
And Appleton's shut up of late,
With 'keep out' signs upon the gate.

Yet here he found his own Eden
Among the sylvan paths untrodden,
Among the birdsong, sedge, and hewel,
The oaks, the elms, the woodlands cool.
Among the ings, the rising Wharfe,
The vision of a world new-morphed
By flooding's flow and ebb, the cattle:
A world imparked, impaled, embattled.

A world within, a world of words,
A world half-real and half-absurd.
A world removed, new-hedged and free
From Worcester, Edgehill, Naseby.
The leaden horrors of that time
Are soothed by Marvell's cadent rhyme,
And we today can also find
A Nun Appleton of the mind.

We never trod that sacred turf
From whence Marvell's poem took its birth.
Be here have pilgrims trod anew,
Found Marvell where the grasses grew.
Here we commune with that great mind,
And, here, our paradise soon find.
Here, where church bells toll the hours,
And cattle play the part of mowers.

Echo is dumb

Without you beside me, echo is dumb as I face what it means
to speak about the century of war and the climb towards peace;
it's not just the wasteland of years between lying open,
their sandstorms of change, their Ozymandias moments:

remember, when the noise retreated,
how in dappled light, stepping straight
our enemies appeared, and, moving
out of the shade, slow and aloof,
dug in their pockets for the measure,
then stretched it twice. Claiming descent
from Andrew Marvell's day, they're reading
out of a page we barely see.

How could I write like him, at home
inside a verse as in a room
securely his by lock and key?
That isn't how verse came to me –
rather, in wounds and desolation;
if calm, the cold of separation.
If I speak hoping to be heard
it must be on a theme that's shared,
but how not fail, miming that voice
that reasoned in the midst of noise?

I may not leave the singular,
Gripping the chart that's served so far.
The mountain roads, knotted and sprawled,
the twisted tree, the waterfall,
are only frames to hold the level
widening perspective of the civil –
but how to step in through the frame?

… I remember, when the map led us to La Verna, we came
climbing past the slim tree-trunks of a forest, once famous for thieves,
to a place we recognised, where the goddess lived who protected fugitives,
and the tailor on pilgrimage recognised you, and St Francis came searching for peace.

To the Lord Protector

> *So restless Cromwell could not cease*
> *In the inglorious Arts of Peace*

At Hinchingbrooke today, beyond the bridge
that only ghosts now use, I took a walk
out of our politics. This 'Country Park'
you knew before the war. We've turned the page

on all that pamphleteering nonsense: kings
and Commonwealth, Tunnage, Poundage, such zeal
for stained glass or fresh air, the sacred call
of hair length. No, we value other things.

Your uncle's home is a school. A hospital's
grown up beside it. Patients sit and wait.
Their blood (so Harvey proved) still circulates
long after Edgehill. Speak, though, of those battles,

or point between our wind-farms to your church
and ask the waiting room what psalms or prayers
are in their heads, or in these jogging cavaliers'
downloaded archives? None. We like to watch

Love Island, not recall the Civil War.
Your statue in St Ives is a convenience
for pigeons, your museum an irrelevance
among the phone shops. What am I calling for

across the ages then? The hornbeams know,
the service trees that cower by the fence
have guessed it, though the A14's advance
has masked so much. I let my pace slow

to look and listen. After all, the border
between the dead and us is not so hard
that you can't whisper, might even be heard.
The gravel pit puts out a call for order.

The reedmace have usurped and falsified
the bulrush name, a revolution stirs
among the lily pads. Then, through all the cars,
through forty decades' dreams of regicide

a sound: of mockery, a laugh that is not
a woodpecker, black-and-white or green,
but something deeper in the woods, unseen,
out loud, and now that tap-tap-tapping note

as if to tune an orchestra of laws
about to break themselves. The park is still.
The line goes dead, but there's a sort of trill
far off, more like a purring, from the house

where once your uncle entertained King James
whose son you later had... Well, let's not dwell
on what's been scanned much better by Marvell,
but go on walking. If our dreams stayed dreams

then there would be no trouble. Cromwell, you
were trouble, for all your good intent
and skill in arts of war. It's time to plant
the bergamot once more; and we should too.

Portrait of a Man Thought to Be Andrew Marvell

As one put drunk into a Humber keel
taking his chance on high tide's surge and swell,
though soaked through I feel my palms grow clammy
at the thought of Winestead sliding from me.
My mind is sand, the channels that it tills,
the mazy, secret kingdoms that it builds.
Albion's high towers in shadow now
infesting prelates their dark plumage show,
until a man might keep a blade concealed
about himself for who knows what dark need.
Such a man as 'Mr George', who crossed
with me to Holland on some special tryst
and pressed on me a pamphlet much inclined
to warnings on fair liberty's decline.
Nameless men I meet in coffeehouses
keep their wide brims pulled down on their faces
riddling where the root of power might lie,
in pope or potentate – or must it die
if not for their great secret work in hand?
The lords at home will learn of what they plan.
Take signs for wonders. Apocalypse engufled
the great gunpowder keg one day in Delft.
I saw a finch land stunned on a wall-bracket:
the fabric of reality had cracked
and I gone through it. My alias grown vague,
I meet a king in waiting in the Hague
(whose name it is not politic to share),
in whom are wed divine right and forced power.
The man once 'thought to be Marvell' purses
his lips at all these tragedies and farces,
and 'Mr George' picks up a little Dutch
for use at cards, the fishhouse, or at church,

and opening new channels of accord
to pass on what the lords at home report.
But whose will be the kingdom still in shade,
the guests for whom the still-life feast is laid?
The battle scenes show how the navy warred,
the faces on the frigates faint and blurred,
but a girl with a lute or posing with a terrier
unseals the space of an interior:
strange privacies reclaimed like a polder
from an outgrown frame that cannot hold her,
and I, unmoored whether I leave or stay,
feel the ground shift and England slip away.

Afterword – Remembering Andrew Marvell
— *Stewart Mottram*

How should we remember Andrew Marvell today? As a poet, a politician, a champion of religious toleration? Does his writing, and the images and ideas it contains, still resonate four hundred years on, or is Marvell's life and literature now of chiefly historical interest – a witness to a lively, but largely remote period in British history, with little relevance to the now? As we mark Marvell's four-hundredth birthday with this collection of quatercentenary poems, it seems an apt occasion to reflect, not only on the state of Marvell scholarship within university circles, but on Marvell's standing with readers more widely. In doing so, we are in good company with T. S. Eliot and Philip Larkin – both poets who used the occasion of Marvell's milestone anniversaries, in 1921 and 1978, to reflect on and reappraise the value of Marvell's poetry for successive generations of readers. *Companions of his Thoughts More Green* offers a creative response to, rather than a critical reappraisal of Marvell's poetry, and yet within the present collection we can point to particular poems or topics by Marvell – Marvell's green themes and mower poems, for example – that have proven particularly popular as prompts for new poems by our contributors. These are prompts that can help signpost those aspects of Marvell's legacy that continue to resonate with readers today. In what follows, I want first to trace the many afterlives of Andrew Marvell across the intervening centuries between his death in 1678 and our quatercentenary celebrations in 2021. I will then turn to identify some of the key themes discernible within the new poems collected here, using these as the basis for some final reflections on Marvell's continuing resonance with readers, four hundred years on.

* * *

'The tercentenary of the former member for Hull', T. S. Eliot wrote in March 1921, 'deserves not only the celebration proposed by that favoured borough, but a little serious reflection upon his writing'.

So began Eliot's influential reappraisal of Marvell as a lyric poet, one whose reputation, for Eliot, stands on the 'precious liquor' to be squeezed from just 'two or three poems', chiefly 'To his Coy Mistress' and 'The Nymph Complaining for the Death of her Fawn'.[1] The quality Eliot admires in these few poems transcends the partisan or political to encapsulate instead what Eliot saw as the great spirit of seventeenth-century poetry – the quality of 'wit' which, in his essay on 'Andrew Marvell', Eliot famously fails to define. Wit, for Eliot, is a product of learning – 'of European, that is to say Latin, culture' – and is an attempt to apply 'a whole civilisation' of thought and feeling to the production of densely allusive images – the so-called metaphysical conceit – which surprise and delight by giving new insight and expression to everyday experience.[2] For Eliot, Marvell was the master of the metaphysical mode, and his essay marked the rise of Marvell's reputation throughout the twentieth century as an erudite and intellectual, but also in some senses an esoteric and elitist poet. When another Hull poet, Philip Larkin, wrote an essay to mark the tercentenary of Marvell's death in 1978, he saw a poet shaped by Eliot's critical legacy – 'a poet of enigma, of concealed meaning, of alternative explanation, of ambiguous attitude' – and wondered if Marvell's poetry was really as complicated as some critics writing in Eliot's wake had suggested.[3]

While it showcased Marvell's metaphysical conceits, Eliot's essay also had the effect of sidelining Marvell's political writings and parliamentary career – the very aspects of Marvell's legacy which were at the forefront of 'that favoured borough', Hull's, civic celebrations in March 1921. Hull marked the three-hundredth anniversary of Marvell's birth with great civic fanfare, and it was his connections to Hull as an MP and a former student of Hull Grammar School that the corporation chose to celebrate, in a service at Holy Trinity Church (now Hull Minster), a wreath laying ceremony at Marvell's statue, and a public meeting in which the mayor at the time – T. Beecroft Atkinson – praised Marvell as 'the greatest advance advertisement agent Hull ever had'.[4] Marvell's 'wandering statue' has been re-sited several times in and around Hull since its first appearance in the new Town Hall in Lowgate in 1867, as Malcolm Watson's contribution to this anthology, 'The Wandering Statues of Marvell and Larkin', makes clear. Less well known is the fact that the message on the plinth to the statue has also changed over the years.[5] In 1921, the schoolboys captured in one of several photographs to survive from Hull's tercentenary celebrations laid their wreaths at the foot of a statue, then at the junction between George Street and Savile Street, which stood on a plinth celebrating Marvell in exclusively political terms: its inscription memorialises Marvell as 'an incorruptible patriot, a wise statesman, and a zealous and energetic representative of this his native town in parliament'.[6] Significantly absent from the inscription on this original plinth, visible in the 1921 photographs, are the lines from the opening of 'To his Coy Mistress' which were added to the granite plinth on which the statue stands in Hull's Trinity Square today. Where today the statue memorialises the politician and the poet, therefore, the absence of Marvell's lines of poetry from the inscription visible beneath his statue at the time of his tercentenary celebrations in 1921 suggests that Marvell, if an 'advertisement', was in the early twentieth century selling two very different products – on the one hand, he is Eliot's sophisticated, cosmopolitan poet; on the other, he is a politician and 'patriot' from Hull.

It is perhaps unsurprising that a poet dubbed 'Amphibious' in his own lifetime should be subject to shifting afterlives in the twentieth century, and the last decades of that century added new critical colours to this most chameleon of poets.[7] Just as Eliot's 1921 essay launched Marvell's legacy as a lyric poet, so Larkin voiced his views on the limitations of the lyric Marvell at a time when the 1978 tercentenary was prompting a wider reappraisal of the political views expressed in Marvell's lyric poetry, alongside a new appreciation of Marvell's Restoration verse satires, notably the 'Advice-to-a-Painter' poems, and controversial writing. Annabel Patterson's *Marvell: The Writer in Public Life* (first published in 1978) was the first serious study to move beyond the lyric poems, kick-starting interest in the politics behind Marvell's other poems and prose writings. A host of important political studies soon followed, while recent years have seen the publication of a new biography and new editions of Marvell's complete poems and prose, helping assemble a clearer picture of Marvell's life and times and a fuller understanding of his complex political and religious views. This, in turn, has helped forge better links between Marvell the poet, and Marvell the MP from Hull, and while we may still admire, with Eliot, the wit and 'true poetry' present in Marvell's 'Nymph Complaining for the death of her Fawn', we have also learned to read Marvell's pastoral complaint as a political commentary on the death of Charles I and the destruction of England's national church.[8]

The late twentieth-century drive to politicize Marvell's poetry, while departing from the lyric readings of an earlier generation of critics, was also in one sense a return to origins, for political readings of Marvell's poetry abounded in the late seventeenth and eighteenth centuries, sparked just weeks after Marvell's death in August 1678 by the birth of the Exclusion Crisis – the political battle waged by Whigs against Tories to exclude the Catholic heir, James, Duke of York, from succeeding his brother, Charles II, as king. Marvell haunted the crisis in more ways than one: not only was Marvell's poetry co-opted by Whigs as a mouthpiece for their political agenda, Marvell himself became the subject of verse satire, his ghost returning in John Ayloffe's 'Marvell's Ghost' (*c.* 1679) to attack the court party.[9] Marvell's posthumous reputation as a poet also rests almost entirely on the decision to publish *Miscellaneous Poems* – from the press of the erstwhile republican printer, Robert Boulter – at the height of the Exclusion Crisis in 1681.[10] The identification of Marvell's poems with the Whig patriot cause clearly stuck, for Marvell's two eighteenth-century editors and biographers – Thomas Cooke and Edward Thompson – were both Whigs who painted a decidedly partisan picture of Marvell as a 'Most Excellent Citizen' and 'Uncorrupted Member of Parliament'.[11] Bookended by the Whig Marvell of his eighteenth-century editors, and by the renewed appetite among late twentieth-century criticism for Marvell's political verse, it is Eliot's emphasis on Marvell as a voice untainted by partisan politics that begins to look eccentric by comparison.

Or does it? In recent decades, criticism may have departed from Eliot in its attentiveness to the depth of Marvell's immersion within the political currents of his day, but it has also departed from the Whig Marvell of Cooke and Thompson in acknowledging, with Eliot, that Marvell's poetry and prose writing bears witness to the complexity of Marvell's political and religious landscape – that Marvell is not as straightforwardly partisan as Cooke and Thompson would have us believe, and that, to use Eliot's words, 'the sense in which a man like Marvell is a "Puritan" is restricted'.[12] Recent research has revealed that 'Puritanism' itself is a term of great complexity, and that a more nuanced understanding of the dynamic religious landscape of Marvell's Britain and Ireland can in turn help us map Marvell's own particular 'moderate puritan' allegiances along the mid-century protestant spectrum from low to high church, nonconformist to conformist, and Calvinist to Arminian. The recent recognition that Marvell most likely maintained moderate Presbyterian views is in turn helping explain the conundrum of Marvell's early royalism, his famously equivocal political standpoint on the Regicide in 'An Horatian Ode', and his alliance with Presbyterian grandees like Thomas Fairfax, Philip Wharton, and the Earl of Shaftesbury.[13] Recent criticism has crafted a thoroughly political Marvell, but it has also brought nuance and complexity to a political and religious landscape that can no longer be understood in the binary terms of bygone generations, as a battle between Whigs and Tories *avant la lettre*.

Recent decades have also read Marvell's poetry as a mirror for some of the key political preoccupations of our own age, with important studies driving debates about Marvell and gender and Marvell and environment. Marvell's representations of gender and sexuality are as amorphous and enigmatic as his constructions of political identity, and much of the recent interest in gender and sexuality emerges from, and intersects with, political readings of his poems and prose, given that constructs of gender and sexuality often had a political currency in the mid-seventeenth century. Eco-critical readings of Marvell's poetry, popular since at least the turn of the twenty-first century, tend to focus on Marvell's representations of nature, and his imaginative identification with grasshoppers and corncrakes, trees and fawns, in poems including *Upon Appleton House*, 'The Garden', and 'The Nymph Complaining for the Death of her Fawn'. Critical interest in Marvell's green thoughts can often seem too inflected by the environmental politics of today, with the 'green Marvell' readily championed, in Brendan Prawdzik's words, 'as an agent of ecological progress' – a vanguard for our own environmental concerns – without due attention to the imperative to read Marvell's approach to the natural through the social, cultural, and theological frameworks of his day.[14] Balancing the green agenda of readers today with a more nuanced ear attuned to the nature of Marvell's own 'green thoughts' will therefore be crucial to future eco-critical work in Marvell studies.

Crucial, too, is a shift in focus from the 'green' to the 'green-blue Marvell' – an attentiveness, that is, to Marvell as a poet immersed for much of his life in the estuary environments of London and Hull, and a corresponding awareness of how the wateriness of these liminal zones, where land meets sea, seeps into the lines of Marvell's poetry. I first encountered Marvell through poems like 'The Garden' and 'To his Coy Mistress' at grammar school in England in the mid-1990s – a time when Marvell was still being read in schools as Larkin's 'poet of enigma' and 'concealed meaning'. It took my arrival in Hull and encounter with Marvell's boyhood world some fifteen years later for me to appreciate that Marvell was not just a poet of Latin learning but a writer immersed within the 'local': the people, politics, and natural environments of the Humber and wider Yorkshire regions. Many of the poems within the present collection also reflect on Marvell's preoccupations with green spaces and wetlands – with the fragile ecologies of the green-blue worlds Marvell encountered in the Humber estuary, the Cambridge fens, and at Nun Appleton in Lower Wharfedale. Poems like Jon Thompson's 'In a Time of Floods', for example, highlight Marvell's own green-blue preoccupations with flooding, in poems including *Upon Appleton House* and 'The Character of Holland' – poems which reflect on Marvell's experience of living with water challenges within estuary regions that were, and remain, acutely vulnerable in the face of flooding. Marvell's flood-filled landscapes are important witnesses to events that resonate with our own experiences of flooding today.

The poems in this collection therefore stand on their own, as high windows onto some of the most pressing issues of the anthropocene: war, pollution, pesticides, and global heating; but these are poems that also prompt readers to return to the pressing themes of Marvell's original poetry. This is why it is regrettable that young readers today in England and Wales rarely encounter Marvell in schools, most literature written in English before 1789, excepting Shakespeare, having been removed from the revised National Curriculum for English launched in 2014. Yet today, as we live through an environmental crisis of our own making, Marvell's 'green thoughts' are arguably more vital than ever, and the case for why we should continue to read Marvell is as strong as it was when Eliot, writing back in 1921, argued for Marvell's revival on the basis of his utilitarian value for readers: 'we may think about him, if there be need for thinking, for our own benefit, not his'.[15] Remembering Marvell four hundred years on, the poems collected here bear witness to the fact that Marvell's legacy remains a potent force today. It is hard to predict what future generations will make of this multifaceted poet and political writer. Yet while the face Marvell presents to the world is ever changing, his standing and reputation in this, his quatercentenary year, endures. Happy Birthday, Andrew Marvell.

Endnotes

1. T. S. Eliot, 'Andrew Marvell' (1921), in *Selected Prose of T. S. Eliot*, ed. F. Kermode (London: Faber, 1975), 161-71 (161).
2. 'Andrew Marvell', 161, 163.
3. P. Larkin, 'The Changing Face of Andrew Marvell', *English Literary Renaissance*, 9.1 (1979): 149-57 (156)
4. *Andrew Marvell, 1621-1678: Tercentenary Tributes by Augustine Birrell... [et al.]*, ed. W. H. Bagguley (1922).
5. G. Watkins, *Andrew Marvell & His Wandering Statue* (Hull: Kingston upon Hull City Museums and Art Gallery, 1996).
6. 'Photographs relating to sites connected with Andrew Marvell', Hull History Centre, Hull, C DMX/168/11.
7. T. Thorowthistle, *Sober Reflections, or, A Solid Confutation of Mr. Andrew Marvel's Works, in a Letter Ab Ignoto ad Ignotum* (London, 1674), 5.
8. 'Andrew Marvell', 167. For political readings of 'Nymph', see *The Poems of Andrew Marvell*, ed. N. Smith (London: Routledge, 2007), 67.
9. N. von Maltzahn, 'Marvell's Ghost', in *Marvell and Liberty*, ed. W. Chernaik and M. Dzelzainis (Basingstoke: Palgrave Macmillan, 1999), 50-74.
10. A. Marvell, *Miscellaneous Poems* (London: R. Boulter, 1681).
11. E. Thompson, *The Life of that Most Excellent Citizen, and Uncorrupted Member of Parliament, Andrew Marvell*, in Andrew Marvell, *Works*, ed. E. Thompson. 3 vols (1776), 3.433-93.
12. 'Andrew Marvell', 162.
13. See, for example, S. Mottram, *Ruin and Reformation in Spenser, Shakespeare, and Marvell* (Oxford: Oxford University Press, 2019); J. Harris and N.H. Keeble, 'Marvell and Nonconformity', in *The Oxford Handbook of Andrew Marvell*, ed. M. Dzelzainis and E. Holberton (Oxford: Oxford University Press, 2019), 144-63
14. B. Prawdzik, 'Greenwashing Marvell'. *Marvell Studies* 4(1).4 (2019): 1-28 (3).
15. 'Andrew Marvell', 161.

Contributors

Suna Afshan is a poet and translator. She is the editor and director of Pallina Press; co-founder and editor-at-large at *Poetry Birmingham Literary Journal*, and on the editorial board of Broken Sleep Books. Her poetry has appeared in the *TLS, Modern Poetry in Translation, London Magazine, Wild Court, Stand*, and others. Suna's micro-pamphlet *Belladonna* was published by the Broken Sleep Books imprint Legitimate Snack in 2020.

Jason Allen-Paisant is from Coffee Grove in Manchester, Jamaica, and is a senior lecturer in Caribbean Poetry & Decolonial Thought in the School of English at the University of Leeds, where he is also Director of the Institute for Colonial and Postcolonial Studies. His debut poetry collection is *Thinking With Trees* (Carcanet, 2021).

Christopher Arksey is a writer and voice actor living in Hull. His poems are also published in *Full House, Moist Poetry Journal, Porridge, Sledgehammer Lit* and *The York Journal*, and he's currently writing his first poetry pamphlet. He tweets @chrisarksey.

Emily Berry is the author of *Dear Boy* (Faber & Faber, 2013) and *Stranger, Baby* (Faber & Faber, 2017). Her third poetry book, *Unexhausted Time*, appeared in 2022.

Nuzhat Bukhari was born in South Asia and moved to England in childhood. She has also spent a year living in Ireland and in America. She taught literature at Oxford and Cambridge for several years. *Brilliant Corners* (CB Editions, 2021) is her first book and was selected as a Poetry Book Society Recommendation.

Stephanie Burt is Professor of English at Harvard. Her most recent books include *After Callimachus* (Princeton UP, 2020) and *Don't Read Poetry: A Book About How to Read Poems* (Basic Books, 2019), along with *For All Mutants* (Rain Taxi, 2021), and *We Are Mermaids* (Graywolf Press, 2022)

Tom Cook was born in Oldham in 1993 and grew up in nearby Saddleworth. He studied at the universities of Hull and Oxford and is currently writing a doctoral thesis on Shakespeare's poetic development at the Shakespeare Institute. His writing has appeared in *Ambit*, the *New Statesman*, *PN Review*, the *Spectator*, the *Times Literary Supplement* and elsewhere.

Ian Duhig's most recent book is his *New and Selected Poems* (Picador 2021) which was awarded the Hawthornden Prize for Literature.

Alec Finlay is an artist and poet. Much of his work considers how we as a culture, or cultures, relate to landscape and ecology. Finlay received the 2020 Cholmondeley award for services to poetry and established morning star publications in 1990. He has published over forty books and won seven Scottish Design Awards, including two Grand Prix Awards (2001, 2015). Recent publications include *a far-off land* (2018); *gathering*, published by Hauser & Wirth (2018), and *th' fleety wud* (2017). He is currently designing Scotland's Covid Memorial.

Cliff Forshaw is a poet and painter. Collections include *Vandemonian* (Arc, 2013), *Pilgrim Tongues* (Wrecking Ball, 2015) and *Satyr* (Shoestring, 2017). *Re:Verb,* a narrative sequence about Rimbaud, and *French Leave: versions and perversions*, are published/due from Broken Sleep Books in 2022/23. http://www.cliff-forshaw.co.uk/

Matthew Francis is the author of seven poetry collections, most recently *Wing* (Faber, 2020), as well as two novels and a collection of short stories. His poetry has twice been shortlisted for the Forward Prize, and in 2004 he was chosen as one of the Next Generation poets. He is the editor of W.S. Graham's *New Collected Poems*, and author of a critical study of Graham, *Where the People Are*. He lives in Wales with his wife, Creina, and is Professor in Creative Writing at Aberystwyth University.

John Greening is the author of more than twenty collections, including *Hunts: Poems 1979-2009* (Greenwich Exchange, 2009), *Omniscience* (Broken Sleep, 2022), and *The Silence* (Carcanet, 2019). He has also edited the work of Edmund Blunden, Geoffrey Grigson, and Iain Crichton Smith, produced several anthologies, and written studies of Elizabethan Love Poets, Yeats, Hardy, First World War Poets, Edward Thomas and Ted Hughes.

Will Harris is a London-based writer. His debut poetry book *RENDANG* (2020) is published by Granta in the UK and Wesleyan University Press in the US. It was a Poetry Book Society Choice, shortlisted for the T.S. Eliot Prize and won the Forward Prize for Best First Collection. His second book of poems, *Brother Poem*, will be published by Granta in 2023.

Ishion Hutchinson was born in Port Antonio, Jamaica. He is the author of the poetry collections, *Far District* and *House of Lords and Commons*. His awards include the Joseph Brodsky Rome Prize, the Windham-Campbell Prize, and the National Book Critics Circle Award.

Aaron Kent is a working-class writer and publisher, and runs Broken Sleep Books. Aaron was awarded the Awen medal from the Bards of Cornwall for his poetry, and his work has been praised by Gillian Clarke, J. H. Prynne, Andrew McMillan, Andre Bagoo, Vahni (Anthony Ezekiel) Capildeo, Abdul Kadeer El-Janabi and John McCullough. His recent books include the full-length collection *Angels the Size of Houses*, and a collaboration with surrealist artist John Welson, *Requiem for Bioluminescence*.

Angela Leighton is senior research fellow at Trinity College Cambridge. She has published various critical books on nineteenth to twenty-first century literature, most recently *Hearing Things: The Work of Sound in Literature* (Harvard, 2018), as well as five volumes of poetry, most recently *Spills* (2016) and *One, Two* (2021), both with Carcanet.

Ingrid Leonard holds an MA in Writing Poetry from Newcastle University and she is currently studying for a PhD in Poetry at the University of Aberdeen, with a focus on Orcadian. Her work has appeared in the *Beyond the Swelkie* and *Ver Prize 2020* anthologies, *Pushing Out the Boat*, *New Writing Scotland*, *Northwords Now*, *The Interpreter's House*, *The Lumiere Review* and *Brittle Star*.

Born in County Durham, **Martin Malone** now lives in north-east Scotland. He has published three poetry collections: *The Waiting Hillside* (Templar, 2011), *Cur* (Shoestring, 2015), *The Unreturning* (Shoestring 2019) and a *Selected Poems 2005 – 2020: Larksong Static* (Hedgehog 2020). He is an editor at *Poetry Salzburg Review* and a Poetry Ambassador for the Scottish Poetry Library. Website: https://www.martinmalonepoetry.com/

Nyla Matuk is the author of two books of poetry: *Sumptuary Laws* and *Stranger*, and the editor of an anthology, *Resisting Canada*. She has contributed to *New Poetries VI* and the *Best Canadian Poetry in English*, and was a finalist for *The Walrus* Poetry Prize and the Gerald Lampert Award. Her poems have appeared in *The Poetry Review*, *PN Review*, *The New Yorker*, *The Walrus*, *Poetry*, and other magazines in Canada, the U.S., and the U.K.

Mary McCollum's pamphlet *heart on the water* was published by dancing sisters (2016). Her debut full collection *living by the law of light* (dancing sisters 2019) was highly commended in the Forward Prizes.

Stewart Mottram writes chiefly on Andrew Marvell, and his critical works include *Ruin and Reformation in Spenser, Shakespeare and Marvell* (Oxford, 2019). He is Reader in English at the University of Hull.

Paul Muldoon is the Howard G. B. Clark '21 Professor in the Humanities at Princeton, and is the author of fourteen collections of poetry, including *Howdie-Skelp* (Faber, 2021).

Eiléan Ní Chuilleanáin was born in Cork in 1942, and taught at Trinity College, Dublin from 1966 to 2011. She was elected Ireland Chair of poetry (2016-2019), and is editor of the literary journal *Cyphers*. Her *Collected Poems* appeared from Gallery Press in 2020 and from Wake Forest University Press, North Carolina, in 2021. She has published eleven collections as well as academic work on the English Renaissance, and translations of poetry from Irish, Italian and Romanian. *Dánta Antonella Anedda*, poems translated from Italian into Irish, was published by Cois Life in 2019.

Sean O'Brien's eleventh collection of poems, *Embark*, will appear from Picador in November 2022. He has recently translated the collected poems of the Kazakh national poet Abai (CUP, 2020) and edited *This is the Life*, the *Selected Poems* of Alistair Elliot (Shoestring, 2021). He is Emeritus Professor of Creative Writing at Newcastle University.

Jana Prikryl is the author of three books of poems, most recently *Midwood* (Norton, 2022). Born in the former Czechoslovakia, she grew up in Canada and now works as an editor at *The New York Review of Books*.

Justin Quinn was born in Dublin and has lived in Prague for thirty years. He has published several collections of poems and translations from Czech, as well as critical studies of modern poetry.

Camille Ralphs has two published pamphlets, *Malkin: An ellegy in 14 spels* (The Emma Press, 2015), which was shortlisted for the Michael Marks Poetry Award, and *uplifts & chains* (If A Leaf Falls Press, 2020). She is poetry editor at the *TLS* and writes the 'Averse Miscellany' column for *Poetry London*.

Carol Rumens, born in South London, currently living in North Wales, has published a number of poetry collections, including, most recently, *Animal People* (Seren, Cardiff, 2016), *Perhaps Bag: New and Selected Poems* (Sheep Meadow Press, NYC, 2017) and *The Mixed Urn* (Sheep Meadow Press, 2019). Her pamphlet, *Bezdelki/ Small Things* (The Emma Press, Birmingham, UK, 2018) won the Michael Marks Award in 2019 for Best Poetry Pamphlet.

Jon Thompson is a Professor Emeritus of English at North Carolina State University. He is the founding editor of the international online journal *Free Verse: A Journal of Contemporary Poetry & Poetics*, launched in 2001 and also the editor of the single-author poetry series, Free Verse Editions, launched in 2005. His newest project is editing *Illuminations: A Series on American Poetics*.

Rory Waterman's full-length collections, all published by Carcanet, are: *Tonight the Summer's Over* (2013; PBS Recommendation, shortlisted for a Seamus Heaney Award); *Sarajevo Roses* (2017; shortlisted for Ledbury Forte Prize for Second Collections); and *Sweet Nothings* (2020). He is on the English faculty at NTU.

Malcolm Watson is an artist and award-winning poet who was encouraged to continue writing poetry by Philip Larkin while studying English at Hull University. He lives in Hull with his family.

David Wheatley's poetry collections include *The President of Planet Earth* (Carcanet, 2017). He recently coedited *The Cambridge History of Irish Women's Poetry* with Ailbhe Darcy, and his novel *Stretto* is published by CB Editions. He lives in rural Aberdeenshire.

LAY OUT YOUR UNREST

www.ingramcontent.com/pod-product-compliance
Lightning Source LLC
Chambersburg PA
CBHW022122040426
42450CB00006B/799